The Key Facts™ on Turkey

Essential Information on Turkey

By Patrick W. Nee

The Internationalist®
www.internationalist.com

The Internationalist®

International Business, Investment, and Travel

Published by:

The Internationalist Publishing Company

96 Walter Street/ Suite 200

Boston, MA 02131, USA

Tel: 617-354-7722

www.internationalist.com

PN@internationalist.com

Copyright © 2013 by PWN

The Internationalist is a Registered Trademark. "Key Facts" and "The Internationalist Business Guides" are Trademarks of The Internationalist Publishing Company.

All Rights are reserved under International, Pan-American, and Pan-Asian Conventions. No part of this book may be reproduced in any form without the written permission of the publisher. All rights vigorously enforced

Table Of Contents

Chapter 1: Background
Chapter 2: Geography
Chapter 3: People and Society
Chapter 4: Government
Chapter 5: Economy
Chapter 6: Energy
Chapter 7: Communications
Chapter 8: Transportation
Chapter 9: Military
Chapter 10: Transnational Issues

Chapter 1: Background

Modern Turkey was founded in 1923 from the Anatolian remnants of the defeated Ottoman Empire by national hero Mustafa KEMAL, who was later honored with the title Ataturk or "Father of the Turks." Under his authoritarian leadership, the country adopted wide-ranging social, legal, and political reforms. After a period of one-party rule, an experiment with multi-party politics led to the 1950 election victory of the opposition Democratic Party and the peaceful transfer of power. Since then, Turkish political parties have multiplied, but democracy has been fractured by periods of instability and intermittent military coups (1960, 1971, 1980), which in each case eventually resulted in a return of political power to civilians. In 1997, the military again helped engineer the ouster - popularly dubbed a "post-modern coup" - of the then Islamic-oriented government. Turkey intervened militarily on Cyprus in 1974 to prevent a Greek takeover of the island and has since acted as patron state to the "Turkish Republic of Northern Cyprus," which only Turkey recognizes. A separatist insurgency begun in 1984 by the Kurdistan Workers' Party (PKK) - now known as the Kurdistan People's Congress or Kongra-Gel (KGK) - has dominated the Turkish military's attention and claimed more than 30,000 lives. After the capture of the group's leader in 1999, the insurgents largely withdrew from Turkey mainly to northern Iraq. In 2004, KGK announced an end to its ceasefire and attacks attributed to the KGK increased. Turkey joined the UN in 1945 and in 1952 it became a member of NATO. In 1964, Turkey became an associate member of the European Community. Over the past decade, it has undertaken many reforms to strengthen its democracy and economy; it began accession membership talks with the European Union in 2005.

Chapter 2: Geography

Location:
Southeastern Europe and Southwestern Asia (that portion of Turkey west of the Bosporus is geographically part of Europe), bordering the Black Sea, between Bulgaria and Georgia, and bordering the Aegean Sea and the Mediterranean Sea, between Greece and Syria

Geographic coordinates:
39 00 N, 35 00 E

Map references:
Middle East

Area:
total: 783,562 sq km
country comparison to the world: 37
land: 769,632 sq km
water: 13,930 sq km

Area - comparative:
slightly larger than Texas

Land boundaries:
total: 2,648 km
border countries: Armenia 268 km, Azerbaijan 9 km, Bulgaria 240 km, Georgia 252 km, Greece 206 km, Iran 499 km, Iraq 352 km, Syria 822 km

Coastline:
7,200 km

Maritime claims:
territorial sea: 6 nm in the Aegean Sea; 12 nm in Black Sea and in Mediterranean Sea
exclusive economic zone: in Black Sea only: to the maritime boundary agreed upon with the former USSR

Climate:
temperate; hot, dry summers with mild, wet winters; harsher in interior

Terrain:
high central plateau (Anatolia); narrow coastal plain; several mountain ranges

Elevation extremes:
lowest point: Mediterranean Sea 0 m

highest point: Mount Ararat 5,166 m

Natural resources:
    coal, iron ore, copper, chromium, antimony, mercury, gold, barite, borate, celestite (strontium), emery, feldspar, limestone, magnesite, marble, perlite, pumice, pyrites (sulfur), clay, arable land, hydropower

Land use:
    arable land: 26.21%
    permanent crops: 3.94%
    other: 69.84% (2011)

Irrigated land:
    53,400 sq km (2012)

Total renewable water resources:
    211.6 cu km (2011)

Freshwater withdrawal (domestic/industrial/agricultural):
    total: 40.1 cu km/yr (14%/10%/76%)
    per capita: 572.9 cu m/yr (2008)

Natural hazards:
    severe earthquakes, especially in northern Turkey, along an arc extending from the Sea of Marmara to Lake Van
    volcanism: limited volcanic activity; its three historically active volcanoes; Ararat, Nemrut Dagi, and Tendurek Dagi have not erupted since the 19th century or earlier

Environment - current issues:
    water pollution from dumping of chemicals and detergents; air pollution, particularly in urban areas; deforestation; concern for oil spills from increasing Bosporus ship traffic

Environment - international agreements:
    party to: Air Pollution, Antarctic Treaty, Biodiversity, Climate Change, Desertification, Endangered Species, Hazardous Wastes, Ozone Layer Protection, Ship Pollution, Wetlands
    signed, but not ratified: Environmental Modification

Geography - note:
    strategic location controlling the Turkish Straits (Bosporus, Sea of Marmara, Dardanelles) that link Black and Aegean Seas; Mount Ararat, the legendary landing place of Noah's ark, is in the far eastern portion of the country

Chapter 3: People and Society

Nationality:
>noun: Turk(s)
>
>adjective: Turkish

Ethnic groups:
>Turkish 70-75%, Kurdish 18%, other minorities 7-12% (2008 est.)

Languages:
>Turkish (official), Kurdish, other minority languages

Religions:
>Muslim 99.8% (mostly Sunni), other 0.2% (mostly Christians and Jews)

Population:
>80,694,485 (July 2013 est.)
>
>country comparison to the world: 17

Age structure:
>0-14 years: 25.9% (male 10,682,900/female 10,201,965)
>
>15-24 years: 17% (male 6,979,955/female 6,703,689)
>
>25-54 years: 42.7% (male 17,375,544/female 17,097,927)
>
>55-64 years: 7.9% (male 3,189,731/female 3,169,450)
>
>65 years and over: 6.6% (male 2,422,983/female 2,870,341) (2013 est.)

Median age:
>total: 29.2 years
>
>male: 28.8 years
>
>female: 29.6 years (2013 est.)

Population growth rate:
>1.16% (2013 est.)
>
>country comparison to the world: 100

Birth rate:
>17.22 births/1,000 population (2013 est.)
>
>country comparison to the world: 109

Death rate:
>6.11 deaths/1,000 population (2013 est.)
>
>country comparison to the world: 160

Net migration rate:
>0.48 migrant(s)/1,000 population (2013 est.)
>
>country comparison to the world: 67

Urbanization:
>urban population: 70% of total population (2010)
>
>rate of urbanization: 1.7% annual rate of change (2010-15 est.)

Major cities - population:
>Istanbul 10.378 million; ANKARA (capital) 3.846 million; Izmir 2.679 million; Bursa 1.559 million; Adana 1.339 million (2009)

Sex ratio:
>at birth: 1.05 male(s)/female
>
>0-14 years: 1.05 male(s)/female
>
>15-24 years: 1.04 male(s)/female
>
>25-54 years: 1.02 male(s)/female
>
>55-64 years: 1.01 male(s)/female
>
>65 years and over: 0.84 male(s)/female
>
>total population: 1.02 male(s)/female (2013 est.)

Maternal mortality rate:
>20 deaths/100,000 live births (2010)
>
>country comparison to the world: 140

Infant mortality rate:
>total: 22.23 deaths/1,000 live births
>
>country comparison to the world: 84
>
>male: 23.29 deaths/1,000 live births
>
>female: 21.12 deaths/1,000 live births (2013 est.)

Life expectancy at birth:
>total population: 73.03 years
>
>country comparison to the world: 126
>
>male: 71.09 years
>
>female: 75.07 years (2013 est.)

Total fertility rate:
>2.1 children born/woman (2013 est.)
>
>country comparison to the world: 110

Health expenditures:

6.7% of GDP (2010)

country comparison to the world: 93

Physicians density:

1.45 physicians/1,000 population (2008)

Hospital bed density:

2.5 beds/1,000 population (2009)

Drinking water source:

improved:

urban: 100% of population

rural: 99% of population

total: 100% of population

unimproved:

urban: 0% of population

rural: 1% of population

total: 0% of population (2010 est.)

Sanitation facility access:

improved:

urban: 97% of population

rural: 75% of population

total: 90% of population

unimproved:

urban: 3% of population

rural: 25% of population

total: 10% of population (2010 est.)

HIV/AIDS - adult prevalence rate:

less than 0.1%; note - no country specific models provided (2009 est.)

country comparison to the world: 159

HIV/AIDS - people living with HIV/AIDS:

4,600 (2009 est.)

country comparison to the world: 120

HIV/AIDS - deaths:

fewer than 200 (2009 est.)

country comparison to the world: 102

Obesity - adult prevalence rate:

27.8% (2008)

country comparison to the world: 36

Children under the age of 5 years underweight:

3.5% (2004)

country comparison to the world: 101

Education expenditures:

2.9% of GDP (2006)

country comparison to the world: 145

Literacy:

definition: age 15 and over can read and write

total population: 87.4%

male: 95.3%

female: 79.6% (2004 est.)

School life expectancy (primary to tertiary education):

total: 12 years

male: 12 years

female: 11 years (2008)

Unemployment, youth ages 15-24:

total: 18.4%

country comparison to the world: 68

male: 17.1%

female: 20.7% (2011)

Chapter 4: Government and Key Leaders

Country name:
    conventional long form: Republic of Turkey
    conventional short form: Turkey
    local long form: Turkiye Cumhuriyeti
    local short form: Turkiye

Government type:
    republican parliamentary democracy

Capital:
    name: Ankara
    geographic coordinates: 39 56 N, 32 52 E
    time difference: UTC+2 (7 hours ahead of Washington, DC during Standard Time)
    daylight saving time: +1hr, begins last Sunday in March; ends last Sunday in October

Administrative divisions:
    81 provinces (iller, singular - ili); Adana, Adiyaman, Afyonkarahisar, Agri, Aksaray, Amasya, Ankara, Antalya, Ardahan, Artvin, Aydin, Balikesir, Bartin, Batman, Bayburt, Bilecik, Bingol, Bitlis, Bolu, Burdur, Bursa, Canakkale, Cankiri, Corum, Denizli, Diyarbakir, Duzce, Edirne, Elazig, Erzincan, Erzurum, Eskisehir, Gaziantep, Giresun, Gumushane, Hakkari, Hatay, Igdir, Isparta, Istanbul, Izmir (Smyrna), Kahramanmaras, Karabuk, Karaman, Kars, Kastamonu, Kayseri, Kilis, Kirikkale, Kirklareli, Kirsehir, Kocaeli, Konya, Kutahya, Malatya, Manisa, Mardin, Mersin, Mugla, Mus, Nevsehir, Nigde, Ordu, Osmaniye, Rize, Sakarya, Samsun, Sanliurfa, Siirt, Sinop, Sirnak, Sivas, Tekirdag, Tokat, Trabzon (Trebizond), Tunceli, Usak, Van, Yalova, Yozgat, Zonguldak

Independence:
    29 October 1923 (successor state to the Ottoman Empire)

National holiday:
    Republic Day, 29 October (1923)

Constitution:
    7 November 1982; amended several times; note - amendment passed by referendum 21 October 2007 concerning presidential elections

Legal system:

civil law system based on various European legal systems notably the Swiss civil code; note - member of the European Court of Human Rights (ECHR), although Turkey claims limited derogations on the ratified European Convention on Human Rights

International law organization participation:

has not submitted an ICJ jurisdiction declaration; non-party state to the ICCt

Suffrage:

18 years of age; universal

Executive branch:

chief of state: President Abdullah GUL (since 28 August 2007)

head of government: Prime Minister Recep Tayyip ERDOGAN (since 14 March 2003)

cabinet: Council of Ministers appointed by the president on the nomination of the prime minister

elections: president elected directly for a five-year term (eligible for a second term); prime minister appointed by the president from among members of parliament

election results: on 28 August 2007 the National Assembly elected Abdullah GUL president on the third ballot; National Assembly vote - 339

note: in October 2007 Turkish voters approved a referendum package of constitutional amendments including a provision for direct presidential elections

Legislative branch:

unicameral Grand National Assembly of Turkey or Turkiye Buyuk Millet Meclisi (550 seats; members elected by popular vote to serve four-year terms)

elections: last held on 12 June 2011 (next to be held by June 2015)

election results: percent of vote by party - AKP 49.8%, CHP 25.9%, MHP 13%, independents 6.6%, other 4.7%; seats by party - AKP 326, CHP 135, MHP 53, independents 36; note - only parties surpassing the 10% threshold are entitled to parliamentary seats

Judicial branch:

Constitutional Court; High Court of Appeals (Yargitay); Council of State (Danistay); Court of Accounts (Sayistay); Military High Court of Appeals; Military High Administrative Court

Political parties and leaders:

Democratic Left Party or DSP [Masum TURKER]; Democratic Party or DP [Namik Kemal ZEYBEK]; Equality and Democracy Party or EDP [Ziva HALIS]; Felicity Party or SP [Mustafa KAMALAK] (sometimes translated as Contentment Party); Freedom and Solidarity Party or ODP [Alper TAS]; Grand Unity Party or BBP [Yalcin TOPCU]; Justice and Development Party or AKP [Recep Tayyip ERDOGAN]; Nationalist Movement Party or MHP [Devlet BAHCELI];

Peace and Democracy Party or BDP [Selahattin DEMIRTAS]; Republican People's Party or CHP [Kemal KILICDAROGLU]; Turkey Party or TP [Abdullatif SENER]

note: the parties listed above are some of the more significant of the 61 parties that Turkey had according to the Ministry of Interior statistics current as of May 2009

Political pressure groups and leaders:

Confederation of Businessmen and Industrialists of Turkey or TUSKON [Rizanur MERAL]; Confederation of Public Sector Unions or KESK [Lami OZGEN]; Confederation of Revolutionary Workers Unions or DISK [Tayfun GORGUN]; Independent Industrialists' and Businessmen's Association or MUSIAD [Omer Cihad VARDAN]; Moral Rights Workers Union or Hak-Is [Mahmut ARSLAN]; Turkish Confederation of Employers' Unions or TISK [Tugrul KUDATGOBILIK]; Turkish Confederation of Labor or Turk-Is [Mustafa KUMLU]; Turkish Confederation of Tradesmen and Craftsmen or TESK [Bendevi PALANDOKEN]; Turkish Industrialists' and Businessmen's Association or TUSIAD [Umit BOYNER]; Turkish Union of Chambers of Commerce and Commodity Exchanges or TOBB [M. Rifat HISARCIKLIOGLU]

International organization participation:

ADB (nonregional member), Australia Group, BIS, BSEC, CD, CE, CERN (observer), CICA, D-8, EAPC, EBRD, ECO, EU (candidate country), FAO, FATF, G-20, IAEA, IBRD, ICAO, ICC (national committees), ICRM, IDA, IDB, IEA, IFAD, IFC, IFRCS, IHO, ILO, IMF, IMO, IMSO, Interpol, IOC, IOM, IPU, ISO, ITSO, ITU, ITUC (NGOs), MIGA, NATO, NEA, NSG, OAS (observer), OECD, OIC, OPCW, OSCE, Paris Club (associate), PCA, SELEC, UN, UNCTAD, UNESCO, UNHCR, UNIDO, UNIFIL, UNRWA, UNWTO, UPU, WCO, WFTU (NGOs), WHO, WIPO, WMO, WTO, ZC

Diplomatic representation in the US:

chief of mission: Ambassador Namik TAN

chancery: 2525 Massachusetts Avenue NW, Washington, DC 20008

telephone: [1] (202) 612-6700

FAX: [1] (202) 612-6744

consulate(s) general: Chicago, Houston, New York, Newton (MA)

Diplomatic representation from the US:

chief of mission: Ambassador Francis J. RICCIARDONE, Jr.

embassy: 110 Ataturk Boulevard, Kavaklidere, 06100 Ankara

mailing address: PSC 93, Box 5000, APO AE 09823

telephone: [90] (312) 455-5555

FAX: [90] (312) 467-0019

consulate(s) general: Istanbul

consulate(s): Adana; note - there is a Consular Agent in Izmir

Key Leaders

Pres.	**Abdullah GUL**
Prime Min.	**Recep Tayyip ERDOGAN**
Dep. Prime Min.	**Bulent ARINC**
Dep. Prime Min.	**Besir ATALAY**
Dep. Prime Min.	**Ali BABACAN**
Dep. Prime Min.	**Bekir BOZDAG**
Min. of Agriculture, Food, & Animal Breeding	**Mehmet Mehdi EKER**
Min. of Culture & Tourism	**Omer CELIK**
Min. of Customs & Trade	**Hayati YAZICI**
Min. of Development	**Cevdet YILMAZ**
Min. of Economy	**Mehmet Zafer CAGLAYAN**
Min. of Energy & Natural Resources	**Taner YILDIZ**
Min. of Environment & Urbanization	**Erdogan BAYRAKTAR**
Min. of EU Affairs & Chief Negotiator	**Egemen BAGIS**
Min. of Family & Social Policies	**Fatma SAHIN**
Min. of Finance	**Mehmet SIMSEK**
Min. of Foreign Affairs	**Ahmet DAVUTOGLU**
Min. of Forestry & Water Works	**Veysel EROGLU**
Min. of Health	**Mehmet MUEZZINOGLU**
Min. of Interior	**Muammer GULER**
Min. of Justice	**Sadullah ERGIN**
Min. of Labor & Social Security	**Faruk CELIK**
Min. of National Defense	**Ismet YILMAZ**
Min. of National Education	**Nabi AVCI**

Min. of Science, Industry, & Technology	Nihat ERGUN
Min. of Transport, Maritime Affairs, & Communications	Binali YILDIRIM
Min. of Youth & Sports	Suat KILIC
Governor, Central Bank	Erdem BASCI
Ambassador to the US	Namik TAN
Permanent Representative to the UN, New York	Yasar Halit CEVIK

Flag description:

red with a vertical white crescent moon (the closed portion is toward the hoist side) and white five-pointed star centered just outside the crescent opening; the flag colors and designs closely resemble those on the banner of Ottoman Empire, which preceded modern-day Turkey; the crescent moon and star serve as insignia for the Turks, as well as being traditional symbols of Islam; according to legend, the flag represents the reflection of the moon and a star in a pool of blood of Turkish warriors

National symbol(s):

star and crescent

National anthem:

name: "Istiklal Marsi" (Independence March)

lyrics/music: Mehmet Akif ERSOY/Zeki UNGOR

note: lyrics adopted 1921, music adopted 1932; the anthem's original music was adopted in 1924; a new composition was agreed upon in 1932

Economy ::TURKEY

Economy - overview:

Turkey's largely free-market economy is increasingly driven by its industry and service sectors, although its traditional agriculture sector still accounts for about 25% of employment. An aggressive privatization program has reduced state involvement in basic industry, banking, transport, and communication, and an emerging cadre of middle-class entrepreneurs is adding dynamism to the economy and expanding production beyond the traditional textiles and clothing sectors. The automotive, construction, and electronics industries, are rising in importance and have surpassed textiles within Turkey's export mix. Oil began to flow through the Baku-Tbilisi-Ceyhan pipeline in May 2006, marking a major milestone that will bring up to 1 million barrels per day from the Caspian to market. Several gas pipelines projects also are moving forward to help transport Central Asian gas to Europe through Turkey, which over the long term will help address Turkey's dependence on imported oil and gas to meet 97% of its energy needs. After Turkey experienced a severe financial crisis in 2001, Ankara adopted financial and fiscal reforms as part of an IMF program. The reforms strengthened the country's economic fundamentals and ushered in an era of strong growth - averaging more than 6% annually until 2008. Global economic conditions and tighter fiscal policy caused GDP to contract in 2009, but Turkey's well-regulated financial markets and banking system helped the country weather the global financial crisis and GDP rebounded strongly to 9.2% in 2010, as exports returned to normal levels following the recession. Growth dropped to approximately 3% in 2012. Turkey's public sector debt to GDP ratio has fallen to about 40%, and at least one rating agency upgraded Turkey's debt to investment grade in 2012. Turkey remains dependent on often volatile, short-term investment to finance its large trade deficit. The stock value of FDI stood at $117 billion at year-end 2012. Inflows have slowed because of continuing economic turmoil in Europe, the source of much of Turkey's FDI. Turkey's relatively high current account deficit, uncertainty related to monetary policy-making, and political turmoil within Turkey's neighborhood leave the economy vulnerable to destabilizing shifts in investor confidence.

GDP (purchasing power parity):

$1.125 trillion (2012 est.)
country comparison to the world: 17
$1.093 trillion (2011 est.)
$1.007 trillion (2010 est.)
note: data are in 2012 US dollars
GDP (official exchange rate):

$783.1 billion (2012 est.)

GDP - real growth rate:

3% (2012 est.)
country comparison to the world: 112
8.5% (2011 est.)
9.2% (2010 est.)

GDP - per capita (PPP):

$15,000 (2012 est.)
country comparison to the world: 90
$14,600 (2011 est.)
$13,800 (2010 est.)
note: data are in 2012 US dollars

GDP - composition by sector:

agriculture: 8.9%
industry: 28.1%
services: 63% (2012 est.)

Labor force:

27.11 million
country comparison to the world: 23
note: about 1.2 million Turks work abroad (2012 est.)

Labor force - by occupation:

agriculture: 25.5%
industry: 26.2%
services: 48.4% (2010)

Unemployment rate:

9% (2012 est.)
country comparison to the world: 104

9.8% (2011 est.)

note: underemployment amounted to 4% in 2008

Population below poverty line:

16.9% (2010)

Household income or consumption by percentage share:

lowest 10%: 2.1%

highest 10%: 30.3% (2008)

Distribution of family income - Gini index:

40.2 (2010)

country comparison to the world: 58

43.6 (2003)

Investment (gross fixed):

21.9% of GDP (2012 est.)

country comparison to the world: 73

Budget:

revenues: $179.9 billion

expenditures: $200.4 billion (2012 est.)

Taxes and other revenues:

23% of GDP (2012 est.)

country comparison to the world: 134

Budget surplus (+) or deficit (-):

-2.6% of GDP (2012 est.)

country comparison to the world: 97

Public debt:

40.4% of GDP (2012 est.)

country comparison to the world: 90

40% of GDP (2011 est.)

note: data cover central government debt, and excludes debt instruments issued (or owned) by government entities other than the treasury; the data include treasury debt held by foreign entities; the data exclude debt issued by subnational entities, as well as intra-governmental debt; intra-governmental debt consists of treasury borrowings from surpluses in the social funds, such as for retirement, medical care, and unemployment; debt instruments for the social funds are sold at public auctions

Inflation rate (consumer prices):

9.1% (2012 est.)
country comparison to the world: 194
6.5% (2011 est.)
Central bank discount rate:

5.25% (31 December 2011)
country comparison to the world: 10
15% (22 December 2009)
Commercial bank prime lending rate:

19% (31 December 2012 est.)
country comparison to the world: 29
17% (31 December 2011 est.)
Stock of narrow money:

$83.29 billion (31 December 2012 est.)
country comparison to the world: 39
$71.95 billion (31 December 2011 est.)
Stock of broad money:

$386.5 billion (31 December 2012 est.)
country comparison to the world: 27
$346.2 billion (31 December 2011 est.)
Stock of domestic credit:

$520.9 billion (31 December 2012 est.)

country comparison to the world: 26
$456.6 billion (31 December 2011 est.)
Market value of publicly traded shares:

$201.8 billion (31 December 2011)
country comparison to the world: 28
$306.7 billion (31 December 2010)
$225.7 billion (31 December 2009)
Agriculture - products:

tobacco, cotton, grain, olives, sugar beets, hazelnuts, pulses, citrus; livestock
Industries:

textiles, food processing, autos, electronics, mining (coal, chromate, copper, boron), steel, petroleum, construction, lumber, paper
Industrial production growth rate:

9.2% (2011 est.)
country comparison to the world: 15
Current account balance:

$-59.74 billion (2012 est.)
country comparison to the world: 189
$-77.24 billion (2011 est.)
Exports:

$154.2 billion (2012 est.)
country comparison to the world: 32
$143.4 billion (2011 est.)
Exports - commodities:

apparel, foodstuffs, textiles, metal manufactures, transport equipment
Exports - partners:

Germany 10.3%, Iraq 6.2%, UK 6%, Italy 5.8%, France 5%, Russia 4.4% (2011)

Imports:

$225.6 billion (2012 est.)

country comparison to the world: 23

$232.9 billion (2011 est.)

Imports - commodities:

machinery, chemicals, semi-finished goods, fuels, transport equipment

Imports - partners:

Russia 9.9%, Germany 9.5%, China 9%, US 6.7%, Italy 5.6%, Iran 5.2% (2011)

Reserves of foreign exchange and gold:

$93.38 billion (31 December 2012 est.)

country comparison to the world: 25

$88.21 billion (31 December 2011 est.)

Debt - external:

$331.4 billion (31 December 2012 est.)

country comparison to the world: 27

$306.7 billion (31 December 2011 est.)

Stock of direct foreign investment - at home:

$117.6 billion (31 December 2012 est.)

country comparison to the world: 35

$102.6 billion (31 December 2011 est.)

Stock of direct foreign investment - abroad:

$21.35 billion (31 December 2012 est.)

country comparison to the world: 45

$19.35 billion (31 December 2011 est.)

Exchange rates:

Turkish liras (TRY) per US dollar -

1.8 (2012 est.)

1.68 (2011 est.)

1.5 (2010 est.)

1.55 (2009)

1.32 (2008)

Fiscal year:

calendar year

Energy ::TURKEY

Electricity - production:

201.2 billion kWh (2010 est.)

country comparison to the world: 22

Electricity - consumption:

155.2 billion kWh (2009 est.)

country comparison to the world: 25

Electricity - exports:

1.918 billion kWh (2010 est.)

country comparison to the world: 41

Electricity - imports:

1.144 billion kWh (2010 est.)

country comparison to the world: 62

Electricity - installed generating capacity:

44.76 million kW (2009 est.)

country comparison to the world: 20

Electricity - from fossil fuels:

65.3% of total installed capacity (2009 est.)

country comparison to the world: 126

Electricity - from nuclear fuels:

0% of total installed capacity (2009 est.)
country comparison to the world: 190
Electricity - from hydroelectric plants:

32.5% of total installed capacity (2009 est.)
country comparison to the world: 68
Electricity - from other renewable sources:

2.2% of total installed capacity (2009 est.)
country comparison to the world: 56
Crude oil - production:

45,740 bbl/day (2011 est.)
country comparison to the world: 61
Crude oil - exports:

0 bbl/day (2009 est.)
country comparison to the world: 194
Crude oil - imports:

284,400 bbl/day (2009 est.)
country comparison to the world: 26
Crude oil - proved reserves:

270.4 million bbl (1 January 2012 es)
country comparison to the world: 58
Refined petroleum products - production:

343,400 bbl/day (2009 est.)
country comparison to the world: 40
Refined petroleum products - consumption:

706,100 bbl/day (2011 est.)
country comparison to the world: 27
Refined petroleum products - exports:

68,450 bbl/day (2009 est.)
country comparison to the world: 51
Refined petroleum products - imports:

297,400 bbl/day (2009 est.)
country comparison to the world: 23
Natural gas - production:

761 million cu m (2011 est.)
country comparison to the world: 68
Natural gas - consumption:

44.71 billion cu m (2011 est.)
country comparison to the world: 22
Natural gas - exports:

713 million cu m (2011 est.)
country comparison to the world: 42
Natural gas - imports:

43.9 billion cu m (2011 est.)
country comparison to the world: 10
Natural gas - proved reserves:

6.173 billion cu m (1 January 2012 es)
country comparison to the world: 85
Carbon dioxide emissions from consumption of energy:

263.5 million Mt (2010 est.)
country comparison to the world: 24

Communications ::TURKEY

Telephones - main lines in use:

15.211 million (2011)
country comparison to the world: 18

Telephones - mobile cellular:

65.322 million (2011)
country comparison to the world: 19

Telephone system:

general assessment: comprehensive telecommunications network undergoing rapid modernization and expansion, especially in mobile-cellular services

domestic: additional digital exchanges are permitting a rapid increase in subscribers; the construction of a network of technologically advanced intercity trunk lines, using both fiber-optic cable and digital microwave radio relay, is facilitating communication between urban centers; remote areas are reached by a domestic satellite system; combined fixed-line and mobile-cellular teledensity is roughly 100 telephones per 100 persons

international: country code - 90; international service is provided by the SEA-ME-WE-3 submarine cable and by submarine fiber-optic cables in the Mediterranean and Black Seas that link Turkey with Italy, Greece, Israel, Bulgaria, Romania, and Russia; satellite earth stations - 12 Intelsat; mobile satellite terminals - 328 in the Inmarsat and Eutelsat systems (2010)

Broadcast media:

Turkish Radio and Television Corporation (TRT) operates multiple TV and radio networks and stations; multiple privately owned national television stations and up to 300 private regional and local television stations; multi-channel cable TV subscriptions available; more than 1,000 private radio broadcast stations (2009)

Internet country code:

.tr

Internet hosts:

7.093 million (2012)

country comparison to the world: 16

Internet users:

27.233 million (2009)

country comparison to the world: 15

Transportation ::TURKEY

Airports:

98 (2012)

country comparison to the world: 61

Airports - with paved runways:

total: 89

over 3,047 m: 16

2,438 to 3,047 m: 35

1,524 to 2,437 m: 17

914 to 1,523 m: 17

under 914 m: 4 (2012)

Airports - with unpaved runways:

total: 9

1,524 to 2,437 m: 1

914 to 1,523 m: 4

under 914 m: 4 (2012)

Heliports:

20 (2012)

Pipelines:

gas 10,706 km; oil 3,636 km (2010)

Railways:

total: 8,699 km

country comparison to the world: 23

standard gauge: 8,699 km 1.435-m gauge (1,928 km electrified) (2008)

Roadways:

total: 352,046 km

country comparison to the world: 19

paved: 313,151 km (includes 2,010 km of expressways)

unpaved: 38,895 km (2008)

Waterways:

1,200 km (2010)

country comparison to the world: 59

Merchant marine:

total: 629

country comparison to the world: 18

by type: bulk carrier 102, cargo 281, chemical tanker 80, container 42, liquefied gas 6, passenger 2, passenger/cargo 60, petroleum tanker 25, refrigerated cargo 1, roll on/roll off 29, specialized tanker 1

foreign-owned: 1 (Italy 1)

registered in other countries: 645 (Albania 1, Antigua and Barbuda 7, Azerbaijan 1, Bahamas 3, Barbados 1, Belize 16, Brazil 1, Cambodia 15, Comoros 8, Cook Islands 4, Curacao 5, Cyprus 1, Dominica 1, Georgia 14, Italy 4, Kazakhstan 1, Liberia 16, Malta 233, Marshall Islands 70, Moldova 18, Panama 62, Russia 101, Saint Kitts and Nevis 18, Saint Vincent and the Grenadines 13, Sierra Leone 9, Slovakia 1, Tanzania 13, Togo 4, Tuvalu 1, unknown 3) (2010)

Ports and terminals:

Aliaga, Ambarli, Diliskelesi, Eregli, Izmir, Izmit (Kocaeli), Mercin (Icel), Limani, Yarimca

Military ::TURKEY

Military branches:

Turkish Armed Forces (TSK): Turkish Land Forces (Turk Kara Kuvvetleri), Turkish Naval Forces (Turk Deniz Kuvvetleri; includes naval air and naval infantry), Turkish Air Force (Turk Hava Kuvvetleri) (2010)

Military service age and obligation:

19-41 years of age for male compulsory military service; 18 years of age for voluntary service; 15 months conscript obligation for non-university graduates, 6-12 months for university graduates; Turkey is trying to reduce dependency on conscription, as of 2004, 75% of soldiers were conscripts; women serve in the Turkish Armed Forces only as officers; reserve obligation to age 41; under a law passed in November 2011, men aged 30 and older who have worked 3 years in foreign countries may pay $16,200 in lieu of mandatory military service (2010)

Manpower available for military service:

males age 16-49: 21,079,077
females age 16-49: 20,558,696 (2010 est.)
Manpower fit for military service:

males age 16-49: 17,664,510
females age 16-49: 17,340,816 (2010 est.)
Manpower reaching militarily significant age annually:

male: 700,079
female: 670,328 (2010 est.)
Military expenditures:

5.3% of GDP (2005 est.)
country comparison to the world: 14
Military - note:

the ruling Justice and Development Party (AKP) has incrementally asserted its supremacy over the military since first taking power in 2002 and has reduced the role of the Turkish Armed Forces (TSK) in internal security, increasing the responsibility of the Turkish National Police (TNP) in combating its Kurdish insurgency; the TSK leadership continues to play a role in politics and considers itself guardian of Turkey's secular state; primary domestic threats are listed as fundamentalism (with the definition in some dispute with the civilian government), separatism (Kurdish discontent), and the extreme left wing; Ankara strongly opposed establishment of an autonomous Kurdish region; an overhaul of the Turkish Land Forces Command (TLFC) taking place under the "Force 2014" program is to produce 20-30% smaller, more highly trained forces characterized by greater mobility and firepower and capable of joint and combined operations; the TLFC has taken on increasing international peacekeeping responsibilities, and took charge of a NATO International Security Assistance Force (ISAF) command in Afghanistan in April 2007; the Turkish Navy is a regional naval power that wants to develop the capability to project power beyond Turkey's coastal waters; the Navy is heavily involved in NATO, multinational, and UN operations; its roles include control of territorial waters and security for sea lines of communications; the Turkish Air Force adopted an "Aerospace and Missile Defense Concept" in 2002 and has initiated project work on an integrated missile defense system; Air Force priorities include attaining a modern deployable, survivable, and sustainable force structure, and establishing a sustainable command and control system (2008)

Transnational Issues ::TURKEY

Disputes - international:

complex maritime, air, and territorial disputes with Greece in the Aegean Sea; status of north Cyprus question remains; Syria and Iraq protest Turkish hydrological projects to control upper Euphrates waters; Turkey has expressed concern over the status of Kurds in Iraq; in 2009, Swiss mediators facilitated an accord reestablishing diplomatic ties between Armenia and Turkey, but neither side has ratified the agreement and the rapprochement effort has faltered; Turkish authorities have complained that blasting from quarries in Armenia might be damaging the medieval ruins of Ani, on the other side of the Arpacay valley;

Refugees and internally displaced persons:

refugees (country of origin): 11,322 (Iraq) (2012); 316,195 (Syria) (2013)

IDPs: 954,000-1.2 million (displaced from 1984-2005 because of fighting between Kurdish PKK and Turkish military; most IDPs are Kurds from eastern and southeastern provinces; no information available on persons displaced by development projects) (2006)

Illicit drugs:

key transit route for Southwest Asian heroin to Western Europe and, to a lesser extent, the US - via air, land, and sea routes; major Turkish and other international trafficking organizations operate out of Istanbul; laboratories to convert imported morphine base into heroin exist in remote regions of Turkey and near Istanbul; government maintains strict controls over areas of legal opium poppy cultivation and over output of poppy straw concentrate; lax enforcement of money-laundering controls

www.ingramcontent.com/pod-product-compliance
Lightning Source LLC
Chambersburg PA
CBHW070733180526
45167CB00004B/1734